THIS JOURNEY BELONGS TO

(And therefore, thanks to the universal laws of journeying, is hereby protected from all judgment, fear, doubt, worry, nay-says, no-ways, and all other forms of internal bullying both conscious and subconscious.)

Published and distributed by Knock Knock
11111 Jefferson Blvd. #5167
Culver City, CA 90231
knockknockstuff.com
Knock Knock is a registered trademark of Knock Knock LLC

ISBN: 978-168349365-5
UPC: 82570350186-5

10 9 8 7 6 5 4 3 2 1

DEAR ME: I LOVE YOU

ACTIVITY BOOK & JOURNAL

KNOCK KNOCK®
LOS ANGELES, CALIFORNIA

CONGRATULATIONS!

You are the you you were given. You are the only you you will ever have. You didn't say "yes," and there is no dress, but you somehow ended up here with you—your only, really, truly forever person. (Go on, you can take a minute to tell your significant other.)

Now, if you and you are going to continue to be together forever and ever, don't you and you deserve to have the kind of relationship people brag about on social media? The kind that celebrates messy hair and mis-sung song lyrics? A relationship that, at the very least, isn't a minefield of criticism, doubt, and insults forged in the locker room of a Midwestern middle school?

The answer, sans dress, is YES.

You deserve pure, unconditional love from yourself—and you deserve to have a you who constantly demonstrates that love, in a million billion trillion little ways. You deserve to cut yourself some slack, give yourself the benefit of the doubt, and stay up late reminding yourself of all your unsung, underappreciated talents. In other words, you deserve the treatment you're already freely giving to your friends, family members, and first dates.

Self-love doesn't have to be ooey or gooey or painted onto a seashell in a dreamcatcher store. It can just be meeting yourself right here, exactly where you are, and being content to sit there together. No pressure. No judgment. No prob.

And self-care doesn't necessarily result in bubble baths and nail salons. It can be the way you ask yourself what you really need—and then meet those needs with zero guilt, because you understand that you deserve to be a fully functioning human with a fully charged battery.

There are no limits to the ways you can show up for yourself. And the best news is, you have an entire lifetime to practice and perfect those ways. The only real requirement is that you start to try.

Self-love is the seed. Self-care is the water. And a happy, secure, I'm-a-truly-unique-badass-human-who-can-do-anything-I-put-my-energy-into is hopefully the flower.

Happy gardening.

HEY YOU. I SEE YOU

REAL TALK: ALL WE EVER REALLY WANT (BESIDES THREE DAYS OFF IN A ROW) IS TO TRULY BE *SEEN*. To express our entire rainbow of feelings, quirks, irks, and "isms" and have them all be received with "I hear you, I get you, and I am here to laugh / cry / rage about that with you."

The good news is that you understand your you-ness better than anyone there is (except, oddly, the algorithm that recommends ads on Instagram. Dinosaur pajamas that have been autographed by Laura Dern? *BUY*.) And the also-good news is that you're never gonna leave you, you don't need a phone to call you, and you're on the exact same schedule as you.

Use this chapter to reconnect with the friend in you, and remember exactly what's there to be seen, heard, and gotten.

DEAR ME: I'm truly a complex mystery, and wow am I thankful for that. With so much to unpack, unravel, and understand, this life isn't getting boring anytime soon...

DEAR ME: I am absolutely allowed (and encouraged!) to feel more than one feeling at a time. I can be sad about something and still be happy overall. I can be mad and in love, frustrated and proud, embarrassed and brave, and any other hodgepodge combination my brain and heart feel like conspiring on. Life is a strange and tangled journey—who am I to try and limit such infinitude?

INTERVIEW WITH A "ME"

Exactly what kind of *you* are you? What do you love, or hate, or frequently Google? And when's the last time you saw it all in writing?

This lil' section is all about sidling up to yourself for some capital Q and T (aka Quality Time!). It's a chance to both speak your truth and to listen to/value your answers. Pretty cool two-birds trick, eh?

So pull up a chair and enjoy this exclusive, hard-hitting interview with yourself. Honesty is encouraged— juicy tidbits welcome!

What are some things that make you feel happy?

A fired-up, totally jazzed–level happy:

_____

_____

_____

A calm, content, favorite-blanket-cozy kind of happy:

_____

_____

_____

What are some things that make you feel the opposite of that?

Like sad . . .

_____

_____

Or angry . . .

_____

_____

Or moderately worried . . .

_____

_____

What would you like to wave your wand and add more of to the world?

(Yup, you can name a bunch! That's the great thing about wands!)

_____

_____

_____

_____

What would you and your wand make less-to-none-of in the world?

_____

_____

_____

What do you value in a good friend?

_____

_____

What do you daydream about?

_____
THE GOOD

_____
THE BAD

_____
THE RANDOM

What would you like to be known for?

_____

_____

Who would you love to meet?

_____
FOR A COCKTAIL OR A COFFEE OR A DECAF SUGAR-FREE ICED TEA

_____
FOR A WEEKEND IN A REMOTE AND 'GRAM-WORTHY PLACE

_____
FOR JUST LONG ENOUGH TO TELL THEM HOW AWESOME THEY ARE BEFORE AWKWARDLY RUNNING AWAY

If you were a non-human animal, what would you be and why?

_____

_____

What are some of your favorite places you've visited, and what was so darn special about them?

PLACE	DARN-SPECIAL QUALITIES
PLACE	DARN-SPECIAL QUALITIES
PLACE	DARN-SPECIAL QUALITIES
PLACE	DARN-SPECIAL QUALITIES

What job / career / lifestyle are you living in an alternate reality (that you like as much as or more than your current, actual one?)

_____

_____

Any thoughts on why Alternate You would choose all that?

_____

_____

What haven't you done in a while that you'd like to do again?

_____

_____

What haven't you done in awhile that you'd like to give a whirl?

_____

_____

What haven't you done, that you will continue to not do, because you have nothing to prove and it really doesn't seem like the cup of tea you're looking for?

_____

_____

If you could instantly acquire one skill or talent, it'd be . . .

_____

If you could instantly eliminate one quality, flaw, or habit, it'd be . . .

_____

One word that really sums up your essence:

_____

Or maybe: _____ ? _Or actually, also:_ _____ !

DEAR ME: My voice is the only my voice the world has. So (ahem) let me speak up for a sec about the things that matter most to me...

LIKE ATTRACTS LIKE
(AND THAT, LIKE, PROVES WHAT WE'RE LIKE)

When we think of our favorite friends and familials, our nearest and dearest and always-want-them-here-est, it's easy to rattle off all the things we love about them. And, though we might not be as quick to see those qualities in ourselves, the principal of "like attracts like" means we probably have them too!

So it's time to play detective! For each near 'n' dear person in your life, list one or more of their personality traits that you admire/adore/adhere to. Then, for each trait you list, name a time when you exhibited that very same quality. Voilà! Irrefutable proof of the likable stuff you're made of! *(Note: will not stand up in a court of law.)*

PERSON I LOVE:

_____

Their most lovable trait(s):

_____

_____

_____

A time I showed the same trait(s):

_____

_____

_____

PERSON I LOVE:

_____

Their most lovable trait(s):

_____

_____

_____

A time I showed the same trait(s):

_____

_____

_____

PERSON I LOVE:

_____

Their most lovable trait(s):

_____

_____

_____

A time I showed the same trait(s):

_____

_____

_____

PERSON I LOVE:

_____

Their most lovable trait(s):

_____

_____

_____

A time I showed the same trait(s):

_____

_____

PERSON I LOVE:

_____

Their most lovable trait(s):

_____

_____

A time I showed the same trait(s):

_____

_____

PERSON I LOVE:

_____

Their most lovable trait(s):

_____

_____

A time I showed the same trait(s):

_____

_____

DEAR ME: It's nice to know there's someone on the planet who sees me so completely that I can spend long stretches of time with them and never have to speak a word. (It's me. I'm the one who sees me like that.)

And it's nice to know that when I do want to speak some things, I can say them to me and they'll be safely kept forever. So here it goes, some things I'd like to safely say/admit/vent/process...

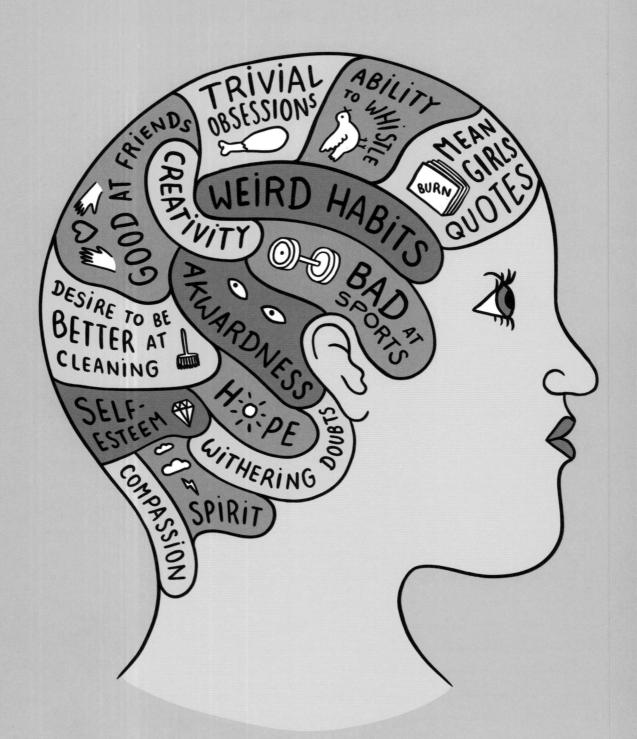

RADICAL SELF-ACCEPTANCE

WE'RE ALL GENERALLY GOOD AT ACCEPTING THINGS IN LIFE THE WAY THEY ARE. When you're eating pizza, you don't say "it's great except it doesn't have a bunch of tacos and sushi on top of it." And when you're driving a car you don't say "but I wish it could also fly." (I mean, sometimes you probably wish it would, but you don't *expect* it to—at least not yet.)

So why should acceptance work any differently when you're applying it to yourself? We all have "flaws" and "imperfections" and "embarrassing things we said to someone we respect that play on an endless loop forever in our brains"... but unless you *radically accept* every part of yourself and your story, you'll forever be focused on the lack of tacos and sushi rather than enjoying your delicious pizza. And that diminishment in energy just might prevent you from inventing flying cars. Wow.

DEAR ME: I am a work in progress. I will always be a work in progress. Every human who has ever lived, at every point in their entire lives, was a work in progress. The key is, we are always making progress...

TOTALLY FLAW·SOME

Here's a quick, random, not-at-all-pointed question to ask yourself (or a "friend"*)...

Is it possible that even my flaws are lovable?

Some Aspects of Me I'd Love to (or Just Maybe Kinda Like to) Change:

1.

2.

3.

4.

5.

*who's yourself

But Actually, When I Think About It…

(Fill in the "***" blanks below with fill-ins from your list opposite!)

When I _____ , it's really coming from a place of
                                        (***)

_____ because I really just want to

_____ .

And the fact that I _____ is actually great, because
                                              (***)

it's kind of what also makes me _____

_____ .

And I can't really celebrate my _____ without also
                                        (A FAVORITE QUALITY, TRAIT, OR TALENT)

accepting _____ , because they're sort of a
                                      (***)

package deal. Both of them are connected to my _____

_____ .

So wait. Can I really harsh on _____ , or is it just a part of what
                                              (***)

it means to be a person who _____

_____ ?

And is _____ really a flaw at all? Or just evidence that
                              (***)

_____ ?

DANG. I guess it is possible. But now what am I gonna get down on myself about?

DEAR ME: I'm always, always doing my best over here, even though "best" can look very different depending on where I'm looking from. A reminder to myself that I was doing my best at the time...

DEAR ME: I have a few personality traits that I wouldn't have chosen. The real choice is: Do I wanna play a bully—who beats myself up about every annoying thing I do? Or do I wanna play a coach—who sees the best in me, and helps me grow, and once in a while jumps up on a bench to make an inspirational speech that ends in a slow clap?

BLAST ~~FROM~~ TO THE PAST

If you have your time machine handy, go ahead and jump in. (If not, then pretend. And make as many beep-boops as you need to.) It's time to take a spin through your past (starting as young as you'd like), and do a little "Tour de You" at all different ages.

These younger you's have a lot to say. They have thoughts and feelings and opinions and concerns . . . but because they are young, they aren't being listened to in the way all those grownups around them constantly are.

What might they say if they knew someone was actually listening?

Give these tinier you's a platform and a voice. Let them speak their minds and air their feelings. This is a safe space for them to rant and rage and carry on. Nothing is too trivial to listen to. They've been waiting patiently to say it for a long time . . .

▼ **AGE:** _____

I hate that . . .
_____
_____
_____
_____
_____
_____

(Wow. Totally get it.)

And it's not fair that . . .

(That sounds hard. You OK?)

I just wish that . . .

(I hear ya, kiddo.)

AGE: _____

I hate that . . .

(Yup. Who wouldn't hate that?)

And it's not fair that . . .

(Yikes. That's wild!)

I just wish that . . .

(Ah, buddy. So understandable!)

▼ **AGE:** _____

I hate that . . .

(Well, yeah. You're sane.)

And it's not fair that . . .

(Geez, that's rough.)

I just wish that . . .

(This is a completely reasonable and relatable sentiment.)

Wouldn't it be cool if we could all go back and help our younger selves? Welp . . . unfortunately we still haven't nailed down the whole space-time continuum thing. So I guess what you can do instead is give yourself this bit of reassurance / hope / rock solid future-guarantee . . .

Dear Me-of-Various-Pasts,

DEAR ME: I'm glad I'm not perfect. Perfect people aren't very fun to be around. Instead, I'll celebrate the things that give me character...

I FORGIVE ME
(AND YOU)
(AND OK FINE, YOU TOO)

FORGIVENESS IS A WONDERFUL WAY TO CLEAN YOUR MENTAL/EMOTIONAL HOUSE AND MAKE SOME ROOM FOR WARMER, FUZZIER FEELINGS. Forgive yourself? Poof! Less doubt and criticism! Forgive others? Blam! Less resentment and anger! Forgive the world at large? Wow! Let's come back to that one after a good night's sleep!

One thing to note: you can forgive without forgetting. Feel free to remember, and learn, and do whatever is needed to adjust... but for your own sanity and growth: forgive anyway.

DEAR ME: Today is a good day to let some thoughts and feelings out.
I'm proud of myself for carrying so many heavy and complicated emotions—
but time to spill a few on the page and give my lower back a break...

DEAR ME: My past is part of my story. The cool thing is, I get to choose how to tell it. (dim lights ... cue orchestra ... release doves ...)

ECHOES FROM THE PAST

The *you* deep inside of you remembers all kinds of echo-y voices from all kinds of specific people in your history. If your life was a movie, these would definitely appear as weird, disembodied floating heads, repeating their little shame-quotes.

Let the *you* deep inside of you tell you all about it. Let them air it out— not in a mean, resentful way. More like in a "I want to say what these people said so I can name it, see it, and send it away" way.

In the word bubbles opposite, write the quotes from your past that get to the crux of all your little whispered I'm-not-worthies. And then feel free to name the people who said them.

Or, if you'd rather keep them anonymous, employ some creative nicknames. Don't worry—"Lord Vegas Douche-ington" isn't going to find your journal.

A BRIEF EPILOGUE...

Look at the names below all those word-bubbles.

How many of those people are people you love / whose opinions you value? (Some of them probably are.) (Lots of them probably aren't.)

For added effect, go ahead and circle the names of the people you still really, really hold in high esteem. Looking at the rest—how much power would you like to give them?

DEAR ME: The best thing about forgiving people is that I get 38.6 percent* of my brain-space back...

*Or up to 12 percent more than that, depending on the size of the transgression and length of time spent stewing.

A BRIEF MOMENT OF FULL·THROTTLE FORGIVENESS

Ahem!

I forgive you, _____

for the echoes of shame you've left in my brain.

I forgive you _____,

and _____,

and _____,

and all of you.

I forgive you because it's compassionate (which I'm told is the sort of evolved emotion I should always aim for) . . . and my compassion reminds me that I've probably caused shame in others, whether I know it or not.

And I forgive you because I'd rather send you on your way than keep clinging to you over and over again. My grip is getting tired.

So best of luck in all your endeavors. Now that I've forgiven you, I can focus my energy on mine.

(Which include: _____

and _____.)

DEAR ME: It's OK for things to be a little hard. If everything were easy, I wouldn't have any stories to tell my grandkids/pets/diary/TED talk audience...

NURTURING MY NEEDS

IS IT OK TO ADMIT YOU HAVE NEEDS? YES! DOES THAT MAKE YOU NEED-Y? NO! You're a living, breathing human being. You have a heart and a brain and a group of friends who are very quick to spoil TV shows if you don't see them right away.

Fulfilling your needs—be they physical (hi, full night's sleep!) or emotional (thanks, phone catch-up with an old friend!) or even totally recreational (I'll never forget you, Harry Potter escape room!)—is an absolutely essential part of feeling good and living a stable life. Here's where you start showing up to actually show yourself that you care . . .

DEAR ME: I am worth every little itty-bitty bit of eensy-weensy decadence I'd like to bestow on myself. Including, but not limited to...

NOTE TO SELF: WRITE SOME NOTES TO SELF!

Fill out the notes below, then cut them out and sprinkle them around the house in places you won't find them right away. Pockets are particularly handy for this assignment, as are backs-of-drawers and zippered-compartments-of-bags. Honestly, without this activity, some of those zippered compartments would probably never be unzipped!

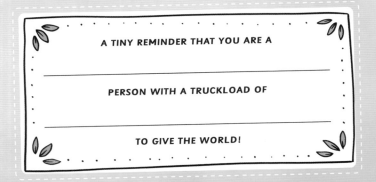

A TINY REMINDER THAT YOU ARE A

_____

PERSON WITH A TRUCKLOAD OF

_____

TO GIVE THE WORLD!

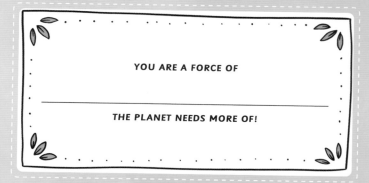

YOU ARE A FORCE OF

_____

THE PLANET NEEDS MORE OF!

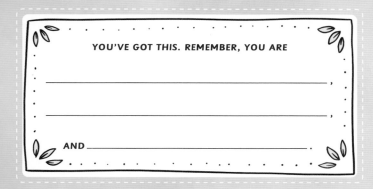

YOU'VE GOT THIS. REMEMBER, YOU ARE

_____ ,

_____ ,

AND _____ .

FEEL LOVED!

I LOVE YOU, BECAUSE YOU'RE SO DARN

_____

3 WORDS TO DESCRIBE THE YOU I KNOW SO WELL:

_____ ,

_____ ,

AND _____ .

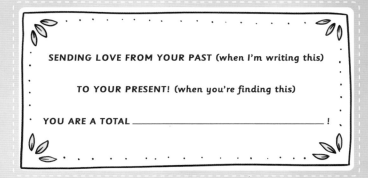

SENDING LOVE FROM YOUR PAST (when I'm writing this)

TO YOUR PRESENT! (when you're finding this)

YOU ARE A TOTAL _____ !

DEAR ME: When the weight of the world is too much, I'm allowed to take a tiny break and delight in some lightness. (Otherwise, I'll be crushed, and then I'm no good to anyone anyway.)

DEAR ME: I'm so grateful for this body that works so hard 24/7-365 to keep me alive. It might be nice to go and do something that will make my body say Thank You to me. Hmmm...

BOUNTIFUL BOUNDARIES!

A COUPLE OF CUTE REMINDERS:

- There's only so much of *you* that you can give to the world before you cease to be healthy (and therefore helpful). Yes, you are a precious resource that needs to be replenished, and you are no good to anyone (least of all you) if you are depleted, downtrodden, or downright cashed.

- You are not obligated to say YES to everything. Sometimes NO is the most positive word in your vocabulary. No, it's true!

- You are *not* being a jerk-wad if you limit your interactions with people who sap your energy, dim your light, abuse your trust, or make you feel less-than. Life is short, and there are plenty of people who are here to support you and conspire to make your best and brightest qualities even better and shinier.

Let the circle below represent a boundary for your life. Inside the circle, write down anything you accept, welcome, and call into your life. (These can be literal things like "paying jobs in the music industry" or "an herb garden." They can also be more general / esoteric things like "adventure" or "gentle vibes.") Outside the circle, write down anything that is no longer welcome. Trust that it will find somewhere else to go that's more aligned with its own journey, and let it wander away while you focus all your goodness on the goodies inside your new life circle.

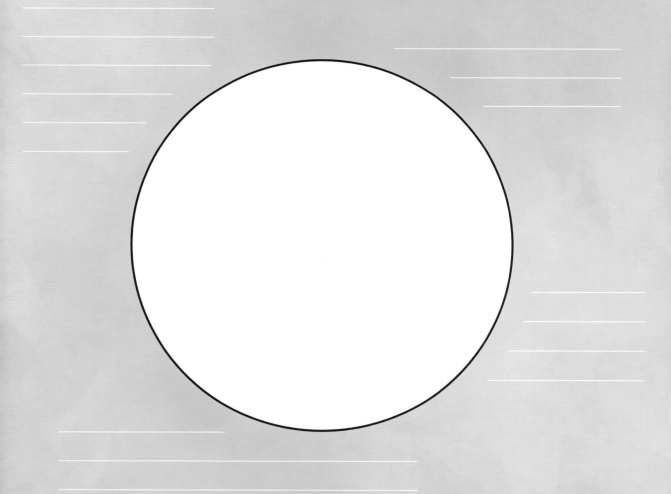

DEAR ME: It's OK if I set goals and don't reach them. And it's alright if I stumble and start over. A goal is a nice compass to have for my road trip— it shouldn't be an obnoxious backseat driver I want to ditch at the first motel...

GRATITUDE
& SHAMELESS SELF·LOVE

NOW THAT YOU'VE MET YOURSELF, ACCEPTED YOURSELF, FORGIVEN YOURSELF, AND FULFILLED YOUR EVERY NEED*, WHAT'S LEFT?

A downright proper celebration. That's right, you deserve to bask in the sunshine at the center of you, and use your gratitude as the fuel that will keep that sun-flame burning bright. This is your permission slip to turn the love cannons on high, and shower yourself with every bit of appreciation, congratulation, and deliciously decadent dispensation you can muster. You're worth every bit of it.

*For the next 2–5 hours. Self-love is a lifelong journey through continually unfolding needs. Welcome!

DEAR ME: I'm leaning into gratitude and seeing beauty in the littlest things. I could lean the other way, but then my beautiful view would be obstructed with crap, and who wants to look at that?

GRATITUDE IS THE ATTITUDE! (ANYBODY WANT A PLATITUDE?)

It's time to throw some logs on the ol' gratitude fire and get those warm and fuzzies burning bright. Having a hard time finding big things to be grateful for? Start small. Can you be grateful you have a functioning mind? A body that keeps you alive? A dirty, disposable gas station lighter that acts as the ghost of spontaneous evenings past, and reminds you of some successful revelry?

Take stock of things you feel thankful for, both big and little. Write down whatever you think of today... and if you think of more later, come back and write those down too. Did you fill up the page? Sounds like a good opportunity to be grateful for all that unused scrap paper...

(**WARNING:** *Doing this for one minute a day may have irreversible effects on your mood and perspective. Those who enjoy living in a cloud of resentment should use this practice with caution.*)

Some little things I'm grateful for:

_____

_____

_____

_____

_____

Some big things I'm grateful for:

_____

_____

_____

_____

_____

Oh yeah, and(!) . . .

_____

_____

_____

_____

_____

⭐ **A TINY NOTE ABOUT GRATITUDE:**

We live in a very upside-down, uneven world, and it can be hard to feel gratitude when we look around and realize that lots of other people don't have the same things we do.

Do not let this turn your gratitude into shame! Fully experience shameless gratitude . . . THEN, also, turn your empathy for others into meaningful action. How can you help those who don't have the same privilege you do? Can you volunteer, donate resources, or otherwise advocate for them?

DEAR ME: I'm beautiful in more than just the basic, boring, traditional way. And my beauty is only getting more beautified with time...

A COMPILATION OF COMPLIMENTATION!

Humility has its place, but it's not welcome on this page. Kindly place it on the shelf, and commence coming up with some not-at-all-humble brags. The harder this is, the more you need to hear it! Don't worry, you're not arrogant . . . and your humility will be right there waiting for you when you're done. #truestory

I am really good at:

And:

And, if I really think about it, also:

When my friends are feeling small or cloudy
or otherwise not-their-best, I'm the one who:

_____

_____

_____

_____

I can always, always be relied upon to:

_____

_____

I have a hidden talent for:

_____

_____

Strangers like that I:

_____

_____

My loved ones like that I:

_____

_____

My pet and/or plants like that I:

_____

_____

The world needs me because it's important to have
people who:

_____

_____

_____

_____

IN OTHER WORDS,
I LIKE ME FOR . . .

These little reasons:

_____

_____

_____

These slightly bigger,
medium reasons:

_____

_____

_____

_____

_____

These very big reasons:

_____

_____

_____

_____

_____

_____

_____

DEAR ME: Scrolling through my memory bank, it's easy to find lots of little, overlooked moments where I was a pretty cool person. Even if no one saw, or mentioned it, or gave me a mug about it...

DEAR ME: Honestly, I love myself just because. (But if I wanna describe that because in gloriously explicit detail, here goes...)

EMBRACING FEAR (OR AT LEAST GIVING IT A CORDIAL HANDSHAKE)

WAIT A MINUTE. LIFE CAN'T BE ALL SHOOTING STARS AND FLYING PONIES AND PIÑATAS FULL OF GRATITUDE, CAN IT?

Nope. No, it can't. Because with great self-love comes great responsibility . . . and that means using your love, gratitude, and fanny pack full of shooting stars to conquer all the nagging voices in your head that say you can't / won't / shouldn't. The greatest act of love you can show yourself is to live your life as fully as you can, *in spite of* all the risks, unknowns, and big-toothed monsters waiting at the door. Make a habit of making friends with fear, and you'll see it's not as scary as you thought.

DEAR ME: Vulnerability might seem scary, but the real HORROR movie would be living a life so full of walls that I never really get to connect...

CONTROL EXPERIMENT

THINGS I CAN CONTROL

THINGS I CAN'T CONTROL

▼ IF I ALLOW MYSELF TO *NOT* BE TOTALLY, COMPLETELY, 100% IN CONTROL
OVER EVERYTHING AT ALL TIMES, MOMENTS, AND MILLISECONDS...

**THESE ARE FEELINGS
I MIGHT FEEL**

**THESE ARE THE WAYS
MY LIFE WILL STILL BE OK**

DEAR ME: Trust might not come naturally, but it's a choice I can make. The cool thing is, it's not only the action, it also becomes the reaction. What a magic trick!

A BRIEF GUIDE TO BLISS·CHASING

There are some things in my life I'd try right now if I weren't worried about what other people might think. BUT! If no one were looking (or judging or opinion-making) all bets would be off! In that case, I'd immediately do / try / explore these things . . .

This is how I'd feel, and what it would do
for me / my psyche / my self-image / my overall sense of well-being…

HMMM . . . SO WHAT'S THE HOLDUP?

Why not try all the stuff right now?
Let's map it out with a very convenient visual aid . . .

▼ **SOMETHING I'M RELUCTANT TO DO:**

_____

_____

RISKS
(ex: People might make fun of me)

REWARDS
(ex: I will feel fulfilled)

VS.

▼ **SOMETHING I'M RELUCTANT TO DO:**

_____

_____

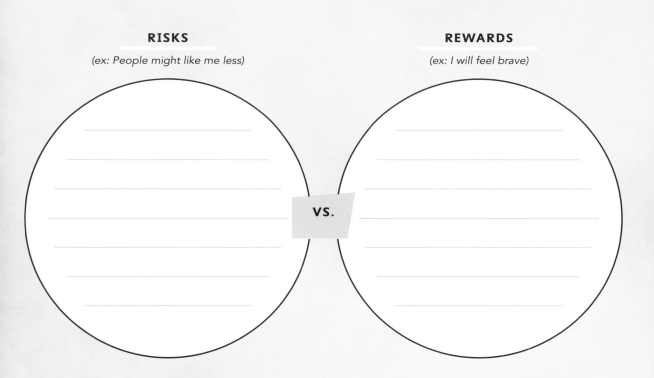

RISKS

(ex: People might like me less)

REWARDS

(ex: I will feel brave)

VS.

Notice that the circles on the left are all about *might*'s, while the ones on the right are about *will*'s. Is it worth sacrificing the guaranteed positives on the right for the uncertain negatives on the left?

DEAR ME: You know what? I might be stronger than I give myself credit for...
(and I'm not talking about the push-ups kind of strong)

DEAR ME: I am safe, and life is short. Let's do this.

AFFIRMATIVE ACTIVATION

CONGRATULATIONS, BEAUTIFUL BEING! NO DOUBT YOU'RE BEGINNING TO GLIMPSE WHAT A SINGULAR JIGSAW PUZZLE OF PERSPECTIVES, TALENTS, AND GIFTS TO THE WORLD YOU ARE.

The important thing now is that you *remember* that fact. Constantly. Relentlessly. Even on bad days. Even in the face of relatives who make you want to chug antifreeze. Even when you open a weird work email that seems to be passive-aggressively calling you out for something in a somewhat public way. Get used to affirming your beauty, your power, your rare and precious you-ness. Because the world only gets one you, and only for a short time . . . you might as well give it the full experience.

DEAR ME: WHEN I'm feeling small, that's a lie. THE truth is, I'm an expansive, RADIANT being capable of anything I want to shine my light on. (But when darkness sneaks up, it's OK to curl up in a ball until the feeling passes through.)

THE GOOD STUFF!*

*(Which I Can Use My Magical Memory Powers to Call Up Anytime, No Phone Required.)

Some good, random times in my life that I've felt...

Supported:

_____

_____

_____

Included:

_____

_____

_____

All-out, full-on celebrated:

_____

_____

_____

Ooh and, let's not forget about my dear friend "PROUD"!

_____

_____

_____

These are some little things I'm proud of:

_____

_____

_____

And some big things I'm proud of:

_____

_____

_____

Mostly, I can be proud that I...

_____

_____

_____

_____

DEAR ME: It is entirely possible to make some (if not all) of my choices based on what will be good for me, what will feed me, what will put my soul in a slingshot and launch it straight into the sky. (Um, sorry about your window, Mrs. Thomas.)

DEAR ME: I have no use for comparison. Their apples are great, my oranges are great...let's all just keep being the best whatever-we-ares we can be.

YOU ARE WHAT YOU SPEAK!

It's probably clear that you can wear down your confidence with negative barbs and insults...(which is why you're going to knock that off and swap all those little nay-sayings for compassion and compliments, right? Good.)

BUT...did you know that you might also be accidentally, subconsciously eroding your confidence and limiting your potential with ordinary turns of phrase that sound completely common and innocent? Crikey! Time to put an end to that too!

Language is power, and words (especially the spoken-out-loud variety) have the ability to color our attitudes and set events in motion for us.

We are constantly, habitually peppering our daily language with the kinds of phrases that keep us small and imply we are needy and/or powerless. *I can't cook...I'm not a reader... I'll never look good in a ten-gallon hat no matter how hard I try.* Wouldn't it be better to constantly declare our worth and power and act as if we had everything we could ever desire (even if we're faking it till we make it)? The answer, of course, is "yeah, duh."

Let's look at the difference in writing.

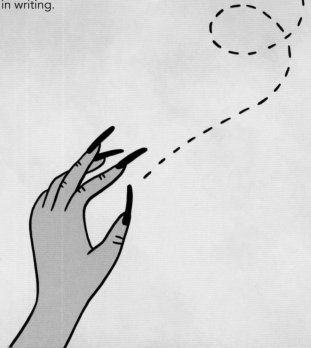

LANGUAGE
THAT KEEPS US SMALL:

I can't

I won't

I'll never

I shouldn't

I'm bad at

I'm not

I hate that I

There's no use

I'm such a screw-up

I wish I could

If only

It's not fair that

Why can't I

Ugh, why am I always so

It's all my fault

LANGUAGE
THAT HELPS US EXPAND:

I am

I have

I enjoy

I claim

I embrace

I begin

I welcome

I love

I burn with

I delight in

I deserve

I celebrate

I attract

I choose

I am grateful for

DITCH THIS:

"I'm bad with money."

TRY THIS:

"I'm learning to be better with money."

DITCH THIS:

"Why can't I find anyone normal to date?"

TRY THIS:

"I'm excited to date a not-at-all-crazy person (and I love that it's a person who also appreciates my references to _____)."

TOTALLY OBSCURE INTEREST

DITCH THIS:

"I wish I had a better job."

TRY THIS:

"I claim my dream job. I enjoy the satisfaction and wealth that it brings me. I love working with people who value me for my unique talents, and I welcome the relaxed dress code that allows me to wear my shark onesie whenever I damn well please. Thank you."

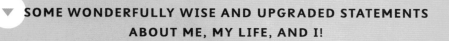

SOME WONDERFULLY WISE AND UPGRADED STATEMENTS
ABOUT ME, MY LIFE, AND I!

The good news is, with a little work, habitual negative language can be given a tune-up and swapped for the kind of juju-inducing phrases that set our train on the right tracks. *(Health, love, and abundance station? All aboard!)* Using the "helps-us-expand" list on the previous page, write some things about yourself and your life. They don't need to be true about your life in *this exact moment.* The act of writing (and saying!) statements that use powerful, expansive language can call whatever it is into being. (Also, wands and potions couldn't hurt.)

DEAR ME: I am a living miracle of consciousness, joy, talent, and love.

How should we celebrate?

ANYWAY, JUST IN CASE YOU HAVEN'T
GOTTEN THE HINT BY NOW . . . I LOVE YOU!

Love, Me